EARTHQUAKE

OTHER BOOKS BY JOHN GABRIEL NAVARRA

Clocks, Calendars, and Carrousels
From Generation to Generation
Our Noisy World
A Turtle in the House
Wide World Weather
The World You Inherit
Nature Strikes Back
Flying Today and Tomorrow
Drugs and Man
Wheels for Kids
Safe Motorboating for Kids
Supercars
Supertrains
Superboats
Superplanes

EARTHQUAKE

John Gabriel Navarra

DOUBLEDAY & COMPANY, INC.
GARDEN CITY, NEW YORK

This book is part of a Museum of Science and Industry/Chicago series of science books published by Doubleday & Company, Inc. The series is designed to inform, stimulate, and challenge youngsters on a wide range of scientific and technological subjects.

Library of Congress Cataloging in Publication Data

Navarra, John Gabriel.
    Earthquake

    "Part of a Museum of Science and Industry/Chicago series of science books."
    Includes index.
    SUMMARY: Discusses the causes, effects, measurement, and prediction of earthquakes. Includes information on earthquake-related problems and how people cope with them.
    1. Earthquakes – Juvenile literature.
    [1. Earthquakes] I. Chicago, Museum of Science and Industry. II. Title.
    QE534.2.N38   551,2'2

ISBN: 0-385-15080-6 Trade
          0-385-15081-4 Prebound
Library of Congress Catalog Card Number 79-8938
Copyright © 1980 by John Gabriel Navarra

Design by Celeste Navarra

PREFACE

Stories about earthquakes have painted into history scenes of fleeing refugees, widespread destruction, and chaos. And so news of an earthquake stirs our imaginations with vivid pictures of devastation that cause us to feel concern for the people in the disaster area.

When you view the aftermath of an earthquake, you get the impression that a giant has seized the buildings and twisted them. The land truly appears as though it has been struck and torn by titanic fingers. It is not surprising that ancient people thought that an earthquake represented the vengeance of the gods.

My purpose is to help you to develop an understanding of the situation and the events that produce the huge dislocations in the Earth's crust that we call *earthquakes*. In this book you will find information about how earthquakes are caused, measured, studied, and predicted. In addition, there is some information about earthquake-related problems and how people cope with them.

JOHN GABRIEL NAVARRA
Farmingdale, New Jersey

CONTENTS

PART 3
PREDICTION AND PROBLEMS 77

ILLUSTRATIONS CREDITS

PART

1

The Restless Earth

In the last ten years, a lot of effort has gone into the development of a theory called *plate tectonics*. This theory seems to explain the underlying cause of earthquakes.

According to the plate-tectonics theory, the surface of the Earth consists of about a dozen giant seventy-mile-thick rock plates. These crustal plates, which are in constant motion, float on the Earth's mantle. The mantle is about 2,000 miles thick and consists of nonmetallic mineral matter called *magma*. The magma on which the crustal plates float is quite hot. Scientists say that the magma is semi-molten.

Each crustal plate is in contact with other plates. The forces propelling the plates cause them to push against one another where they meet. Friction at the edges of plates sometimes temporarily locks two plates in place and causes stresses to build up. Eventually the locked rock fractures under the stress and the plates resume their motion. It is this sudden fracture and release of pent-up energy that causes earthquakes.

1

DRIFTING CONTINENTS

In 1912, Alfred Wegener, a German scientist, proposed that continents are like huge wandering rafts. Wegener's ideas are known as the *hypothesis of continental drift*. He suggested that today's continents originally broke free and floated away from a single landmass called *Pangaea* — shown in the upper drawing, opposite.

Alfred Wegener's hypothesis was the ancestor of the modern theory of plate tectonics. But it took fifty years for his view of the Earth to be generally accepted.

Pangaea, Wegener's universal landmass, is believed to have existed about 200 million years ago. Panthalassà is the ancestral Pacific Ocean. The Tethys Sea is the ancestral Mediterranean. Sinus Borealis is the ancestral Arctic Ocean.

The breakup of Pangaea took place about 180 million years ago. The lower drawing shows the northern group of continents split away from the southern group. The name *Laurasia* identifies the northern group and *Gondwana* identifies the southern group of continents. In fact, you can see that Gondwana has also started to break up. India has been set free. And the Africa-South America landmass has separated from the Antarctica-Australia landmass.

2

A BATTLE OF PLATES

According to the modern plate-tectonics theory of continental drift, magma from the mantle is constantly welling up into the crust. The upwelling is taking place along certain plate boundaries. Magma, for example, is moving into the crust between the Eurasian and North American plates.

The boundary between the Eurasian Plate and the North American Plate is found at the bottom of the Atlantic Ocean. The Eurasian-North American boundary is known as the *Mid-Atlantic Ridge*. This ridge is midway between the western and eastern shores of the Atlantic.

The rising magma that intrudes itself between the plates becomes new crustal material. The creation of new crust along the Mid-Atlantic Ridge is widening the Atlantic Ocean. The Atlantic is widening at the rate of one inch per year. And as a result, the North American Plate is being pushed toward the west while the Eurasian Plate is being pushed toward the east.

The western edge of the North American Plate lies where California and the neighboring Pacific Plate meet. This boundary, or junction, along the California coast is called the *San Andreas Fault.*

The San Andreas Fault is in reality a tear in the Earth's crust. It represents a zone of powerful collision where two great plates are sliding past each other. The sliver of California that is west of the fault is located on the Pacific Plate. The Pacific Plate is moving toward the northwest. The portion of California to the east of the fault is on the North American Plate, which is moving westward.

About 90 per cent of the world's earthquakes take place along plate boundaries. Any sudden movement along the San Andreas Fault causes an earthquake in California. The photo on the following pages was taken after a pent-up energy release along the San Andreas Fault. The overpass has collapsed and the road surface has a tear running across its width.

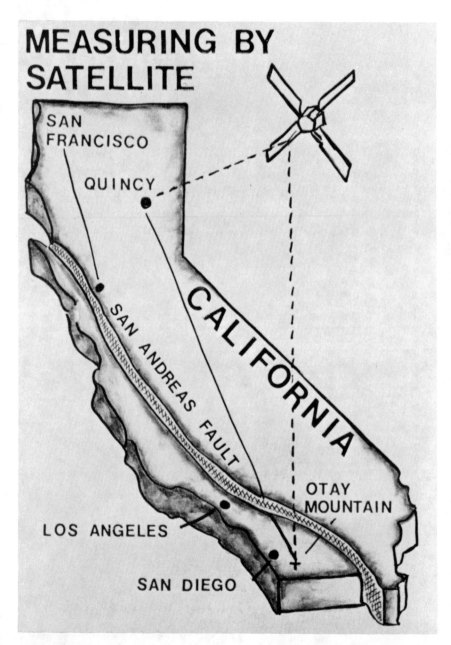

MEASURING BY SATELLITE

SAN
FRANCISCO

QUINCY

CALIFORNIA

SAN ANDREAS FAULT

OTAY
MOUNTAIN

LOS ANGELES

SAN DIEGO

3

TRACKING A FAULT

The San Andreas Fault cuts to the east of Los Angeles and to the west of San Francisco. Los Angeles is on the Pacific Plate, which is moving to the northwest. The motion of the Pacific Plate will eventually place Los Angeles alongside San Francisco.

Scientists predict that the transport of Los Angeles to the San Francisco area will take ten million years. They base this prediction on various estimates and measurements. Studies done before 1972 indicate a relatively steady rate of movement of two inches per year. Measurements made after 1972 reveal a more rapid rate of movement.

In 1972, scientists at the Goddard Space Flight Center in Maryland developed a new system for measuring motion along the fault. They set up two stations on opposite sides of the fault. One station is at Quincy. The other is at Otay Mountain outside San Diego.

A laser device was set up at Quincy and another was set up at Otay. Then from each station a laser beam was directed at a satellite orbiting 600 miles above the Earth. The information provided by this technique allowed the scientists to measure the distance between the stations with great accuracy.

The Goddard scientists made measurements in 1972,

1974, and 1976. Over the four-year period they found that Quincy and Otay moved closer by fourteen inches. This is an average rate of three and one-half inches per year, which is more than anyone had expected.

These new findings indicate far more activity along the fault than previously suspected. It may mean that energy is accumulating at a rapid rate. And because more energy than anticipated is being locked into the rock fractures, its release might produce an enormous earthquake.

The photo below is an aerial view of the San Andreas Fault. The fault is seen as a line that works its way northwestward. The arrow-like mark on the ground in the photo identifies the fault zone.

4

TAKING THE EARTH'S PULSE

An earthquake is a trembling of the ground. Most earthquakes are barely noticeable, but some are violent and destructive. The ground can break apart during a violent earthquake, leaving gaping trenches, the remains of demolished buildings, disrupted roadways, displaced railroad tracks, and dangling power lines.

The point at which the first release of the energy that causes an earthquake occurs is called the *earthquake focus*. The focus generally lies below the surface. The point on the Earth's surface directly above the focus is referred to as the *epicenter*. Scientists describe the location of an earthquake focus by giving the geographic position of its epicenter and its depth.

How is the energy of an earthquake transmitted from the focus to other parts of the Earth? As with any release of energy, vibrations or disturbances spread outward from the focus. The vibrations that go out from an earthquake focus are called *seismic waves*, after the Greek word for earthquake. The seismic waves spread out in all directions from the focus, just as sound waves spread out in all directions when a gun is fired.

Seismic waves are the shakers and wreckers that accompany the release of energy at the focus. There are two general types of seismic waves produced by earthquakes: surface waves and body waves.

Surface waves are so named because they travel along the Earth's surface. They produce most of the destruction because they actually make the ground roll. Surface waves are usually stronger than body waves.

The seismic vibrations called *body waves* are sometimes referred to as *preliminary waves* since they arrive before the surface or rolling waves. There are, however, two different and distinct types of body waves. The first

is classified as a *compression wave*, while the second type is said to be a *shear wave*.

The compression waves produced by an earthquake travel at great speeds. They ordinarily are the first signals indicating that an earthquake has occurred. Since they are the first to arrive, compression waves are referred to as the *primary waves*, or *P waves*.

A *P* wave arrives at the surface like a hammerblow. The blow is the result of energy released deep within the Earth. The blow of a *P* wave travels in the same way that a bump from a locomotive on one freight car travels all the way through a long train.

P waves—like sound waves—move through both liquids and solids by compressing the material directly ahead of them. Each compressed particle, in turn, springs back to its original position as the energy moves on. This event—compression of a particle to its springback—is called a *cycle*. The time within which such a cycle is completed is referred to as the wave's *period*.

The *P* wave is the swiftest seismic wave. Its speed, however, varies with the material through which it passes. *P*-wave velocity in the crust of the Earth usually is less than four miles per second, or 14,000 miles per hour. But just below the crust in the mantle, the speed of a *P* wave jumps to five miles per second, or 18,000 miles per hour. As a *P* wave passes deep into the Earth and moves below the mantle through the core, its speed increases to seven miles per second. Thus, it travels through the Earth's core at more than 25,000 miles per hour.

When a *P* wave strikes an object embedded in the ground, it produces a series of sharp pushes and pulls. These pushes and pulls are in a direction parallel to the wave path. The second type of body wave, on the other hand, produces a shearing effect or a side-to-side shaking of an object embedded in the ground.

The shear waves produced by an earthquake are referred to as *secondary waves*, or S waves. One reason for the shear waves to be called secondary is that they ordinarily reach the surface after the P waves. The shear, or S, waves displace an object at right angles to their direction of travel and are thus sometimes called *transverse waves*.

The S wave must have a rigid medium through which to move. These transverse or shear waves do not travel below the mantle. The outer portion of the Earth's core, which is just below the mantle, is liquid, and S waves cannot travel through it.

Let's stop for a moment and put all of this information together. The first signal you get that an earthquake has occurred will often be a sharp thud. The thud, or ham-

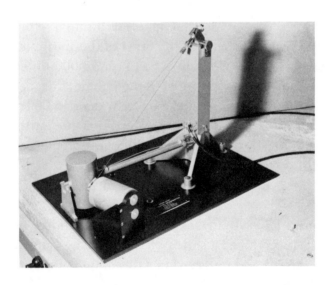

merblow, indicates the arrival of the compression, or *P*, waves. Then the *P* waves are followed by the shear, or *S*, waves. With the arrival of *S* waves, objects begin to shake from side to side. Then, when the surface waves arrive, the ground begins to roll.

The vibrations produced by earthquakes are recorded and measured by instruments called *seismographs*. A variety of different seismographs have been designed because seismic waves have a wide range of periods. Remember, the period of a seismic wave is nothing more than the time within which it completes a cycle. Some waves generated at a focus can have periods that are extremely long. Others have periods of less than a tenth of a second.

Scientists must use different seismographs to record the different waves. Some seismographs are sensitive to short-period waves and others are sensitive to long-period waves. Photos of two seismographs are shown.

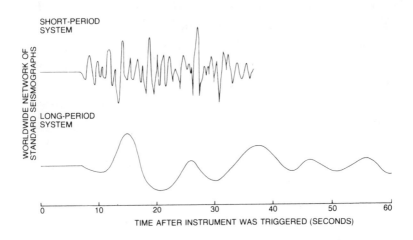

SHORT-PERIOD SYSTEM

LONG-PERIOD SYSTEM

WORLDWIDE NETWORK OF STANDARD SEISMOGRAPHS

TIME AFTER INSTRUMENT WAS TRIGGERED (SECONDS)

The photo on page 24 shows a short-period seismograph. The photo on page 25 shows a long-period instrument. The pair of curves above are the recordings made of one earthquake's *P* wave. The upper curve was recorded by a short-period seismograph. The lower curve was recorded by a long-period seismograph.

The general principle of the seismograph is rather simple. You can see how it operates by trying this: Place a half dollar on a scratch pad held horizontally in your hand. Move the pad suddenly forward and then back. Now, just as suddenly, move the pad sideways and then back. The half dollar tends to remain in one place while the scratch pad slips about under it. A seismograph is nothing more than an instrument that has a weight supported clear of the ground and freely suspended.

When *P*, *S*, and surface waves travel through the Earth to a seismograph, they shake the supports on which the weight hangs. But the weight, because of its inertia, tends to remain steady in one place. A recording needle, or pen, attached to the weight is used to trace a graph on

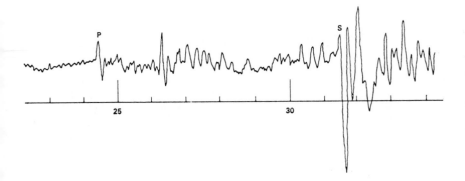

a revolving drum that is attached to the supports of the apparatus. In other words, body waves (*P* and *S*) and the surface waves shake the supports of the seismograph. In turn, the supports shake the revolving drum and the paper on it. Everything shakes except the steady mass of the weight and the pen attached to it. In this way, a pen writes a record of the vibrations.

The zigzag line made by the pen of a seismograph is called a *seismogram*. In the drawing above you see a seismogram recorded by a seismograph located at Florissant, Missouri, a few miles northwest of St. Louis.

The seismogram is marked with a time scale. Each unit on the time scale is one minute. Note the points labeled "*P*" and "*S*" on the seismogram. The points indicate when the *P*-wave trains and the *S*-wave trains begin.

The waves recorded by the seismograph prior to the arrival of the *P*-wave train represent the background vibration that exists at Florissant. This is a continuous record of exceedingly small waves. The small waves are known as *microseisms*. The microseisms are made by disturbances other than earthquakes.

Remember, P and S waves leave the earthquake focus at the same instant. They travel outward in all directions. The fast-moving P waves reach the seismograph first. Then, some time later, the slower-moving S waves arrive. The delay in arrival time is proportional to the distance traveled by the waves. In other words, the farther away the center, or focus, of the earthquake shock is, the longer is the spread of time between the arrival of the P and the S waves.

The data recorded in a seismogram allow the scientists to describe the earthquake. The recorded heights, or amplitudes, of the P, S, and surface waves, for example, indicate the amount of energy released. By combining data from selected seismograph stations, the epicenter and the focal depth of an earthquake can be located.

5

SCALING EARTHQUAKES

In the case of a violent dislocation that produces a severe earthquake, the energy is released in one large wrench followed by smaller tremors. The tremors are referred to as "aftershocks." The aftershocks are produced by the continuing collapse and movement of crustal blocks. Sometimes the violent wrench is preceded by small structural failures that produce foreshocks. The foreshocks are really small tremors.

News about an earthquake nearly always causes a person to ask: What happened to people in the area? Were many buildings destroyed? How severe was the quake? Most reports of such an event include a statement that attempts to rank the earthquake.

At the present time, two scales are used to describe the severity of an earthquake: the Richter scale and the modified Mercalli scale. The Richter and Mercalli scales are completely separate in intent.

The Richter scale measures an earthquake in terms of its energy or magnitude at the moment when it begins. Magnitude is expressed as a number on the Richter scale. The number is derived from the amplitude of the recorded seismic waves. Thus, the Richter scale is based on instrument records.

The second scale, the Mercalli scale, is based on personal observations. The Mercalli scale describes the actual effect or intensity of an earthquake at a particular location. The Mercalli scale is a subjective measure. It describes the damage to life and property.

The Richter magnitude scale gives a measure of the energy released by an earthquake at its point of origin. In order to assign a number on the Richter scale, the measurement must be based on a seismogram made at a distance of sixty-two miles from the epicenter. Most stations that record earthquakes, however, are bound to be at some distance other than sixty-two miles. This means that seismograms from several different stations are studied. Then complex conversion tables are used to arrive at the final or standard number.

The Richter scale actually has no fixed lower or upper limit. It does not rate the size of an earthquake on a scale of 0 through 10. Small earthquakes are measured at figures around zero. Some are recorded as minus numbers of magnitude. An earthquake of magnitude 1 normally can only be detected by a seismograph. The weakest disturbance noticed by people are magnitude 2 earthquakes.

According to the Richter scale a magnitude 5 earthquake releases energy equivalent to that which would be released by 1,000 tons of TNT. A magnitude of 7 on the Richter scale indicates that the energy released is equivalent to about one million tons of TNT. Any earthquake with a Richter value of 6 or more is commonly considered to be a major disturbance. The Alaskan earthquake of March 27, 1964, was described as having a magnitude of 8.5 on the Richter scale.

The modified Mercalli intensity scale grades earthquakes by describing the kinds of damage and effects caused by them. According to the Mercalli scale, an earthquake may vary in intensity from Degree I to Degree XII.

On the Mercalli scale, a Degree I earthquake is not felt except by a few people under especially favorable conditions. A Degree II earthquake is felt by people, and it causes delicately suspended objects to swing. A

Degree IV earthquake cracks walls and produces the sensation that a heavy truck has just struck a building.

A Degree IX rating on the Mercalli scale is given to an earthquake that shifts buildings off foundations and conspicuously cracks them. An earthquake that leaves few, if any, masonry structures standing, destroys bridges, and produces broad fissures in the ground is given a rating of XI on the Mercalli scale. An earthquake with a rating of XII is one in which the damage is total and waves are seen on ground surfaces. The Alaskan quake of 1964 was rated as X on the Mercalli scale. Landslides (shown opposite), rockfalls, and slumps in river banks were part of the destruction caused by the Alaskan quake.

Now, it should be clear that there is a difference between the Richter and the Mercalli scales. An earthquake of large magnitude on the Richter scale may not necessarily cause intense surface effects. In such a circumstance, the earthquake would be given a very low rating on the Mercalli scale.

The effect as measured by the Mercalli scale depends to a large extent on local surface and subsurface conditions. An area underlain by unstable ground such as sand or clay is likely to experience more noticeable surface effects than an area that is equally distant from the epicenter but underlain instead by granite or firm ground.

6

KILLER WAVES

The most damaging aftermath of an earthquake may be the sea waves it produces. Ocean waves generated by an earthquake are called *seismic sea waves*, or *tsunamis*. In other words, a tsunami is the destructive oceanic offspring of an earthquake or seism.

Sometimes tsunamis are erroneously called "tidal waves," but tsunami is the correct name and is used internationally. The word "tsunami" originated with the Japanese, whose islands have felt the destructive power of these terrible killers from the sea for generations.

A large earthquake in the Pacific can create waves capable of flooding villages and cities on the coasts of North and South America, Asia, and the islands in between. The destruction produced by a tsunami can be staggering. A tsunami in 1896 killed 27,000 people in Japan.

The Prince William Sound earthquake of March 27, 1964, was one of the largest shocks ever recorded on the North American continent. Its magnitude on the Richter scale was 8.5. The quake's epicenter was located at approximately 61° N latitude and 148° W longitude. This placed the focus somewhere between Crescent Glacier and Unakwik Inlet.

This earthquake generated tsunamis of record size which destroyed much of Valdez, Alaska. Thirty-one people in Valdez lost their lives. In addition, the waves struck south and produced extensive destruction and loss of life in Crescent City, California. At Crescent City, eleven people lost their lives and an estimated $7.5 million worth of damage was done. The sea waves continued to roll south, passed southern California and Mexico, and then went on to the shores of Chile. The ocean waves produced by the Alaskan earthquake also moved across the Pacific, touching Hawaii and Japan.

In the open ocean, the height of a tsunami or its wave amplitude is very small. At most, a tsunami will not be more than two or three feet high in the open sea. Thus, they cause no problem at all to ships in mid-ocean or well beyond the shoreline.

The wavelength of a tsunami, or the distance from

crest to crest, may be more than 100 miles. If you were on a ship at sea, you would not be aware that a tsunami had passed. In other words, a wave with a height, or amplitude, of two or three feet would roll by; then, fifteen or thirty minutes later, another wave of approximately the same height would follow.

The elapsed time — that is, the time it takes two successive crests to pass a fixed location — is called the *wave period*. The wave period for tsunamis ranges from fifteen to thirty minutes.

The waves of a tsunami do not travel at a uniform speed. The speed at which they move depends upon the depth of the water. A tsunami travels at speeds ranging from about 150 miles per hour in water that is 1,600 feet deep to about 670 miles per hour in water 30,000 feet deep.

While it is true that the amplitude of a tsunami is small in the open ocean, its height from crest to trough changes dramatically as the shore is approached. As the tsunami enters the shoaling water of a coastline, the wave velocity diminishes while its wave height increases. These changes occur because the bottom of the ocean interferes with the movement of the wave.

The tsunami obeys the general laws of wave physics as it "feels" bottom. At a water depth equal to one-half its wavelength, the solid bottom of the sea changes the tsunami's velocity. Frictional drag against the sea floor causes a loss of wave energy and, thus, a decrease in tsunami velocity.

A tsunami moves at a speed of 670 miles per hour when the water depth is 30,000 feet. But when the depth decreases to 24,000 feet, the velocity of the wave drops to 600 miles per hour. In water depths of 18,000 feet, the tsunami travels at a speed of 519 miles an hour. Velocity is cut to 424 miles an hour when it moves across water depths of 12,000 feet. When it encounters bottoms at 6,000 feet, the tsunami slows to 299 miles per hour. In depths of 3,000 feet, its speed is 212 miles per hour, while it moves along at no more than 94 miles per hour through water with a depth of 600 feet. The tsunami speed is slashed to a mere 30 miles per hour in water depths of 60 feet.

Two additional conditions develop as a result of the tsunami's "feeling" bottom. The first is that, as the velocity of the wave decreases, its length will be affected. The wavelength of the tsunami decreases because the following crest begins to draw closer to the crest in front, which is slowing as it "feels" bottom. Then, as a result of the decrease in velocity and wavelength, the wave begins to steepen dramatically. The crest builds to fantastic heights.

The arrival of a tsunami begins with what appears as an abnormally low tide. The coastal waters actually recede because a trough moves in advance of the crest of the initial wave. The low tide develops in a matter of minutes and exposes the ocean floor far beyond the limits of normal low tides. The abnormal lowering of the water level indicates that the steepening tsunami wave is not far behind. The wave, which in the open ocean had an amplitude of a mere three feet, steepens with each decrease in its velocity until it develops amplitudes of more than 100 feet. These tremendous waves strike with a devastating force.

A great gouge in the Earth's crust, called the *Aleutian Trench*, stretches westward more than 2,000 miles from Alaska toward the Kamchatka Peninsula. The Aleutian

Trench is deep beneath the North Pacific Ocean. In places, it runs as deep below sea level as Mount Everest is high above the sea's surface.

On April 1, 1946, a major earthquake in the depths of the Aleutian Trench caused the sea floor to shift. There was an abrupt change in sea level and a tsunami was generated. The Aleutian tsunami moved south across the Pacific toward the Hawaiian Islands.

In the preceding photo we can see the tsunami hitting Hawaii Island. Can you see the man in the lower left-hand corner? When the tsunami arrived, its wave steepened to heights of fifty-five feet. More than 150 lives were lost, 163 people were injured, and 500 homes were demolished by the wave as it moved inland.

The Alaskan earthquake of 1964 triggered many landslides that occurred below the sea surface. The landslides generated local waves in many of the harbors and bays. The local waves proved to be very destructive. The most devastating local waves struck at Seward, Valdez, and Whittier.

At Seward—shown in the photo opposite—a stretch of the waterfront about 3,500 feet long and 300 feet wide, including all of the pier facilities, slid into Resurrection Bay. This slide occurred shortly after the earthquake started and while the shaking was still intense. The slide itself drew water away from the shoreline and created two or its own disturbances at distances of half a mile from the shore. Waves spread in all directions as a result of the landslide. The initial shock of the earthquake had ruptured waterfront fuel storage tanks. The oil from these tanks ignited immediately. The waves generated by the landslide spread the fiery oil throughout the area.

7

COMPUTING AND WARNING

The Aleutian tsunami of 1946 caused major damage and many casualties in the Hawaiian Islands. Our government decided that a means of providing tsunami warnings to the people of Hawaii had to be developed. On August 12, 1948, a plan was approved and the operation of the Tsunami Warning System (TWS) began.

In 1960, ocean waves generated by a quake took a heavy toll of ships along the southern coast of Chile. This Chilean tsunami spread across the Pacific and killed 180 persons in Japan and Okinawa. The destruction caused by the Chilean tsunami of 1960 prompted a large number of countries to join the TWS established by the United States.

Then, in 1964, the great Alaskan earthquake produced a devastating tsunami. Many areas of the Pacific region were affected by the Alaskan tsunami, and the need for an international warning system became apparent.

In 1965, the United Nations accepted the offer of the United States to expand its TWS located at Honolulu. The Honolulu Observatory is now the operational center for the International Tsunami Warning System (ITWS).

The objectives of the ITWS are to detect and locate major earthquakes, determine whether they have created tsunamis, and provide information and warnings to any population that is threatened. The system monitors seismological and tidal installations in Hawaii and other locations around the world. A tsunami watch is issued by ITWS whenever an earthquake with sufficient magnitude to generate a tsunami occurs.

Functioning of the ITWS begins with the detection, by any participating observatory, of an earthquake of sufficient size to trigger the alarm attached to the seismograph at that station. The scientists at the station determine the location of the earthquake epicenter. If the epicenter is under or near the ocean, they know that tsunami development is possible. On the basis of the seismic evidence available to them, the scientists send out a bulletin that indicates that an earthquake has occurred. They broadcast the location of the epicenter and indicate that the possibility of a tsunami exists.

The first positive indication that a tsunami has been generated usually comes from tide stations nearest the disturbance. As soon as they are able to confirm that a tsunami exists, the scientists at the Honolulu center issue a tsunami warning. They immediately announce the estimated time of arrival of the tsunami at all locations.

In 1964, the only system operating was the TWS of the United States. Eight minutes after the beginning of the Prince William Sound earthquake, the P waves it generated reached Hawaii. These P waves, moving through the Earth, triggered the alarm attached to the seismograph at the Honolulu Observatory. The scientists at the observatory went into action. The record of the seis-

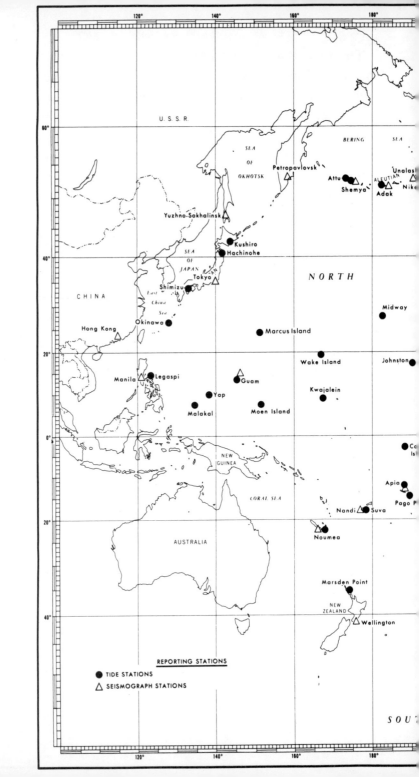

REPORTING STATIONS

● TIDE STATIONS

△ SEISMOGRAPH STATIONS

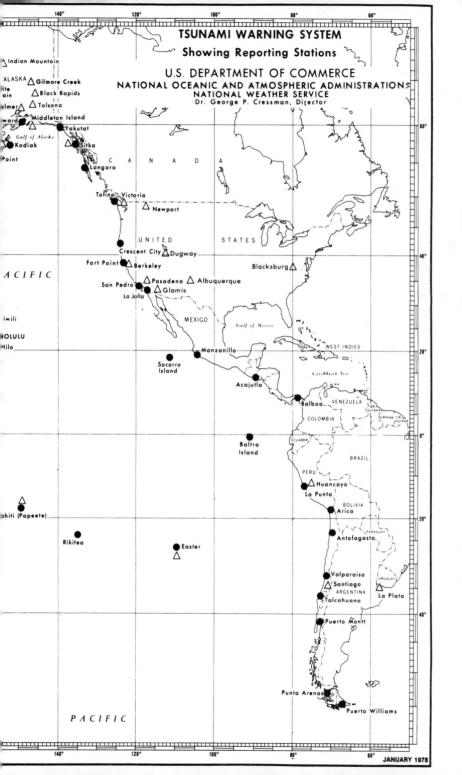

mogram was examined immediately, and the Hawaiian civil defense authorities were notified of the earthquake.

The observatory in Honolulu sent requests for seismic readings to various observatories throughout the world. The first seismic report received from another observatory was from Manila. It gave the P-wave reading at the Manila Observatory. In a short time, enough information had been received to permit the Honolulu Observatory to locate the earthquake epicenter. The Honolulu Ob-

servatory immediately computed the estimated arrival time of the tsunami for various locations in the Pacific.

The Canadian government, in July 1963, withdrew from the TWS that began functioning in 1948. Thus, no official warning of the tsunami was provided to Canada, since it had been out of the system for almost a year by March 1964. Unfortunately, the tsunami from the Alaskan earthquake of 1964 struck the Canadian coast near the time of high tide. The tsunami, coupled with the

47

water levels of high tide, produced extensive destruction. The twin cities of Alberni and Port Alberni sustained the most damage. The highest wave reported in Canada was at Shields Bay on the west coast of Graham Island. The crest was almost thirty-two feet high and the waves severely damaged a logging camp.

The tragedy in Canada was compounded by the lack of Canadian interest in being a part of the TWS. The twin cities of Alberni and Port Alberni are about thirty-five miles from the open ocean at the head of the long, narrow Alberni Inlet. The tsunami moved up this narrow passageway and swept into the towns.

The effect of the first wave was devastating. The worst flooding conditions in the area had never caused anything like the damage of the tsunami. The second crest of almost twenty-one feet was the highest. But, fortunately, because of the shape of the Alberni Inlet, the period from the first to the second crest was ninety-seven minutes. Thus, after the initial wave hit, the inhabitants of these Canadian cities were alert to the danger that would most certainly follow. In the hour and a half before the second crest arrived, many of them left the low-lying areas and got to safer positions on higher ground.

The great seismic sea waves cannot be stopped. But the damage they produce can be minimized and people can live through the disaster by following these safety rules:

■ Not all earthquakes cause tsunamis, but many do When you hear that an earthquake has occurred, stand by for a tsunami emergency.

- An earthquake in your area is a natural tsunami warning. Do not stay in low-lying coastal areas after a local earthquake.

- A tsunami is not a single wave, but a series of waves. Stay out of danger areas until an "all-clear" is issued by a competent authority.

- Approaching tsunamis are sometimes heralded by a noticeable rise or fall of coastal water. This is nature's tsunami warning, and it should be heeded.

- A small tsunami at one beach can be a giant a few miles away. Don't let the modest size of one make you lose respect for all.

- The International Tsunami Warning Center does not issue false alarms. When a warning is issued, a tsunami exists. The tsunami of May 1960 killed sixty-one people in Hilo, Hawaii, who thought it was "just another false alarm."

- All tsunamis—like hurricanes—are potentially dangerous, even though they may not damage every coastline they strike. Tsunami damage to a port area is shown in the photo opposite.

- Never go down to the beach to watch for a tsunami. When you can see the wave, you are too close to escape it.

- Sooner or later, tsunamis visit every coastline in the Pacific. Warnings apply to you if you live in any Pacific coastal area.

- During a tsunami emergency, your local Civil Defense, police, and other emergency organizations will try to save your life. Give them your fullest cooperation.

PART
2

Portraits of Catastrophe

Although some countries seem to be struck more than others, no nation is a safe haven beyond the reach of earthquakes. As we look back over the years it is appalling to read about the devastation caused by these disasters. The death toll caused by some quakes is impressive: Corinth, Greece, in the year 856, 45,000 died; Shensi, China, in 1556, 830,000 people perished; Calcutta, India, during 1737, 300,000 died; Lisbon, Portugal, in 1755, 60,000 people died.

In this century, we have had more than our share of earthquakes. The following is a very short list of some of the great twentieth-century quakes: Martinique (1902), San Francisco (1906), Kansu, China (1920), Tokyo (1923), Agadir, Morocco (1960), Alaska (1964) (photos opposite show a J. C. Penney store before and after a quake), Peru (1970), Managua, Nicaragua (1972), Tang-Shan, China (1976), and Iran (1978).

When quake centers are marked on a map, it becomes clear that most earthquakes occur along plate boundaries. The Pacific Plate, for example, is neatly outlined by the earthquake-marked "ring of fire" around the Pacific. But earthquakes can occur well within a plate, too.

8

SHOCKS WITHIN PLATES

Earthquakes do occur well within a plate. The reason for an earthquake occurring far from a plate boundary is not always clear. Sometimes the plate structure has been weakened in those places during ancient periods of volcanic activity. But an earthquake, wherever it occurs, is always the result of stress that builds and is released in one pent-up surge.

Charleston is a city on the eastern coast of South Carolina. It is in an active earthquake region. Although Charleston is at the edge of the Atlantic Ocean, this city is more than 1,000 miles from the edge of the North American Plate. Remember, the eastern edge of the North American Plate is at the Mid-Atlantic Ridge, which divides the Atlantic in half.

Charleston was hit by a major quake on August 31, 1886. The photograph taken just after the earthquake struck shows the kind of damage that occurred. The quake left much of the city in rubble. The shock was felt over two million square miles — as far away as Chicago and Boston. Approximately sixty people were killed in the city of Charleston as a result of this quake.

Some people say that America's greatest earthquake struck on December 16, 1811. It, too, occurred far from a

plate boundary. The quake hit in the heartland of the United States at the frontier Mississippi River town of New Madrid, Missouri.

At two o'clock in the morning, the 800 inhabitants of New Madrid were roused from their sleep by a thunderous shock. The shock struck with such force that trees snapped, split, and fell. Long, low swells passed through the ground like ocean waves. Great fissures opened in the land and swallowed homes. The mighty Mississippi River boiled, foamed, and spread over most of New Madrid.

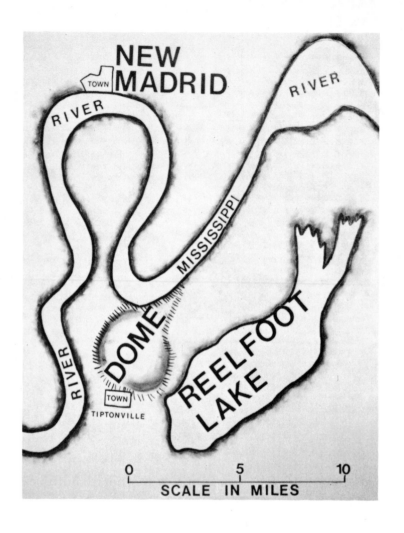

SCALE IN MILES

From its epicenter in New Madrid, the earthquake sent its waves north and south along the Mississippi River Valley. The waves struck east and west. Chimneys fell in Tennessee, Georgia, South Carolina, and Virginia. Tremors were felt as far away as Boston.

Shocks continued almost daily. The shocks that struck on January 23 and February 7, 1812, were almost as vio-

lent as the initial shock of December 16, 1811. In fact, the last shock of the series hit in March of 1822 — a little more than ten years after the first.

Fifty thousand square miles of land were affected by the New Madrid earthquakes. Some of the changes produced by the earthquakes are visible today. One stretch of land — about twenty-five square miles — was raised about twenty feet. Today it is called the *Tiptonville Dome*.

Reelfoot Lake, shown above, was created by the New Madrid earthquake. Prior to the quake the Reelfoot Lake region was a swampy area fed by creeks. During the earthquake, the swampy region sank. Then an adjacent area was thrust upward and this cut off the creeks' outlet. The creek water flowing into the newly sunken swamp had no outlet and it accumulated to form Reelfoot Lake.

During the earthquake the mighty Mississippi was thickened with mud and silt thrown up from its bed. It churned and tore at its banks. At one point, pressures deep underground exploded through the riverbed from bank to bank. The upheaval hurled a huge wall of water upstream. For a short time the Mississippi River flowed backward!

The shocks and the upheavals forced the Mississippi to establish new channels in some locations. When the earthquake ended, the river was flowing over much of New Madrid. The present town of New Madrid was built by the survivors of the quake on the relocated riverbank.

9

NEW ENGLAND EARTHQUAKES

It comes as no surprise to anyone that more than seventeen million Californians live within a major earthquake region. But it does come as a surprise to most New Englanders that more than three million of them live in a major earthquake-risk zone. The outline of New England shows where major earthquakes have occurred in the past. Information for New York, Pennsylvania, and New Jersey is also included on the map.

One of New England's most recent tremors occurred in June of 1973. It shook the ground throughout the region. The region's last major quake, however, struck on Christmas Eve in 1940. The quake was rated as having a magnitude of 6 on the Richter scale. The intensity level on the Mercalli scale was VII — houses shook, plaster and chimneys fell.

The epicenter of the Christmas 1940 earthquake was in central New Hampshire. Its location in New Hampshire is shown on the map on page 59 as a black triangle. The quake's rating — on the Richter as well as the Mercalli scale — established it as a major earthquake.

During the past 300 years many tremors have occurred in the New England region. The pattern of these tremors has led some scientists to identify a 200-mile-wide corridor that stretches from Boston, Massachusetts, to Ottawa, Canada, as an area of high risk. The corridor, which stretches in a northwesterly direction, is marked on the map. It is called the *Ottawa-Boston trend.*

Forty-two black triangles are shown on the map. Each represents the epicenter of a major earthquake that has occurred. Some of these quakes have been rated as being above VIII on the Mercalli scale.

The first New England earthquake to become part of our written record struck in June of 1638. It was described by William Bradford of the Plymouth Colony. From the descriptions, the 1638 quake would have been rated as VIII on the Mercalli scale.

The 1638 earthquake was the first to occur after the Pilgrims landed. But there were others before the colonists arrived. The Indians told the settlers about precolonial tremors. At least four tremors occurred in the eighty years prior to 1638.

A trembling off Cape Ann, Massachusetts, in 1755 produced the first eastern earthquake of note. It struck before dawn on the morning of November 18, 1755. The shocks were felt from Nova Scotia to Chesapeake Bay. The disturbance was especially strong around Boston. Wooden and masonry buildings were destroyed. A considerable number of landslides occurred and fractures in the ground appeared in many communities.

Note that there are three black triangles in the ocean off Cape Ann. This means that three major earthquakes had their epicenters in this location. The first trembling off Cape Ann was recorded in 1727. The 1727 earthquake was felt as far away as Philadelphia. The third quake off Cape Ann took place in 1925. A lengthy series

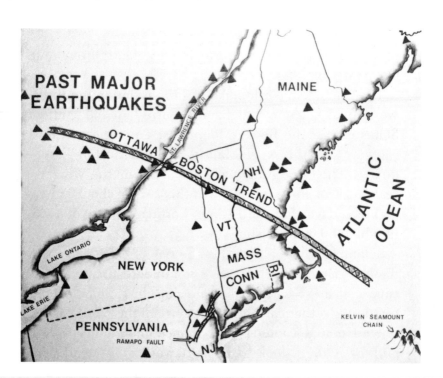

of tremors was felt in eastern New England throughout the winter of 1925.

The Cape Ann earthquake of 1755 is one of the three worst quakes known to have occurred in the United States east of the Rocky Mountains. The others in this category are the New Madrid and Charleston earthquakes. The Cape Ann quake reached X on the Mercalli scale. It is of some interest that this severe shock struck eighteen days after the Lisbon, Portugal, quake of 1755 in which 60,000 perished.

Scientists now believe that the risk of earthquakes in the New England region has been underestimated. The causes of these earthquakes are not clear. Some scientists believe that earthquake activity in the Northeast is related to huge cooled pillars of once-molten rock called *plutons*. Others look to the Ottawa-Boston trend and suggest that it is an extension of the Kelvin Seamount Chain that lies off the Atlantic coast. They relate the *seamount chain* and the Ottawa-Boston trend to an unseen instability in the crust.

Still other scientists simply believe that the cause of New England earthquakes is linked to the most recent ice age. During its southward push and northward retreat some fourteen thousand years ago, the last glacier affected the Northeast. The crust in the region was depressed, or downwarped, as a result of the great mass of ice on it. Now, the New England crust, these scientists say, is readjusting itself to a weight loss that resulted from the melting of glacial ice. Some parts of the New England coast have risen 100 feet above sea level during this period of adjustment. This slow readjustment of the crust to new "weighting" conditions may be causing earthquakes.

10

A HAWAIIAN EARTHQUAKE

The largest island of the Hawaiian chain, Hawaii, was struck by an earthquake at dawn on the morning of November 29, 1975. The epicenter is shown on the map. Its location is on the southeastern coast along a fault zone on the side of the Kilauea volcano.

The earthquake was rated as having a magnitude of 7.2 on the Richter scale. Earthquake intensities from III through VIII on the Mercalli scale were felt at various locations. The zone of maximum damage—VIII on the Mercalli scale—is shown on the map. The Degree VIII zone stretches from the Puna district northeastward to the city of Hilo. This was the greatest Hawaiian earthquake in over a century.

The major shock was preceded by numerous foreshocks. Some of the foreshocks had magnitudes between 5 and 6 on the Richter scale. Large-scale ground movements accompanied the quake. In addition, a series of rockfalls from the island's steep cliffs were triggered by the foreshocks and the main shock.

Within a minute of the main shock, a surging wave, a tsunami, struck the beach. Twenty-one people were

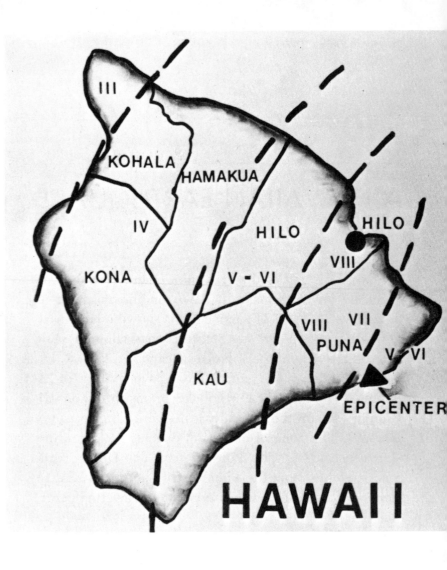

camping on the beach at the time. The wave washed trees rocks, and people into a twenty-foot-deep crack that opened. The tsunami's height was about thirty-six feet. Fortunately, it only swept inland for slightly more than 300 feet.

The ground movements triggered a brief eruption at the summit of the Kilauea volcano. The summit area of Kilauea dropped by at least three feet. The drop resulted from a migration of magma beneath the summit reservoir to unknown sites within Kilauea's fault zone. A thousand or more earthquakes per day continued to shake the region for two weeks after November 29.

11

QUAKES ALONG FAULTS

About two-thirds of the earthquakes in the United States occur along the faults of the Pacific coast. The California earthquake of April 18, 1906, is one of the most notable. More than 700 lives were lost and most of San Francisco was destroyed.

Within San Francisco, buildings (photo opposite) and the water supply system were demolished. Fires broke out after the quake. The city burned for days because there was no water to control the fires.

The 1906 earthquake was the result of movement and readjustment along the San Andreas Fault. This fault, remember, is a zone of collision between the Pacific Plate and the North American Plate. The San Andreas Fault extends from Imperial Valley, just north of the Mexican border, northwestward through the coastal ranges to Golden Gate Gorge. A short distance north of Golden Gate, the fault passes out to sea through Tomales Bay.

Another major earthquake belt that results from the collision of plates extends in an arc across southeastern and southern Asia into southern Europe. This zone extends into the eastern Mediterranean. Iran and Turkey

are located along the belt. The faults in the Iranian and Turkish regions mark zones of collision between the African and Eurasian plates.

On September 6, 1975, a strong earthquake was triggered by movement along the Anatolian Fault that slashes across Turkey. The noontime quake toppled buildings and killed at least 1,000 people in eastern Turkey. Aftershocks continued past midnight.

The general location of the Anatolian Fault is shown on the map below. The 1975 quake caused by movement along this fault measured 6.8 on the Richter scale. It was a very devastating tremor. The earthquake produced damage throughout eastern Turkey and in provinces along the Black Sea. The photo opposite shows a Turkish village destroyed by the quake.

Earthquakes along the Anatolian Fault in Turkey have taken more than 40,000 lives since 1939. The fault has been the epicenter for more than fifteen major earthquakes in forty years. Eleven of these earthquake epicenters have been located on the map below.

On September 16, 1978, a devastating shock struck along the earthquake belt that runs through Iran. The epicenter of the quake was located at Tabas, an agricultural center in eastern Iran. Tabas is on the edge of the central Iranian desert. The city is 400 miles southeast of Tehran. It is close to Iran's border with Afghanistan.

The 1978 Iranian quake was measured at 7.7 on the Richter scale. Of Tabas's 17,000 people, as many as 15,000 perished within the first minute of the quake's onset. The shock was felt with destructive effects in two-thirds of Iran. More than forty villages within a radius of sixty miles of the epicenter were completely leveled. The quake was strong enough to rock buildings in Tehran, 400 miles from the epicenter.

The same general region in Iran had been struck ten years earlier, on August 31, 1968. The 1968 earthquake had a Richter scale reading of 6.5. It killed 12,000 people. The death toll from 1978's massive earthquake was more than 25,000.

12

TREMORS FROM TRENCHES

On May 21, 1960, a series of severe earthquakes struck southern Chile. Ten days of terror left more than 5,700 people dead and 350,000 homeless. More than 65,000 dwellings were destroyed.

The quake's epicenter was located in the Peru-Chile Trench just to the west of the city of Concepción. The first shock lasted a mere thirty-five seconds. But within this brief span of time, one-third of the buildings in Concepción collapsed.

Three major shocks struck on May 22. The tremors and destruction continued for eight more days. Some 800 miles of canals and waterways — as far south as the Strait of Magellan — were disrupted. Islands disappeared and new islands appeared.

The lower diagram opposite shows what is happening along the west coast of South America. The Nazca Plate is plunging under the South American Plate. The crunch and collision of the plates created the Andes, a mountain chain that runs along the length of Chile's western coast.

The South American Plate offers a lot of resistance to the plunging plate. Enormous friction builds along the

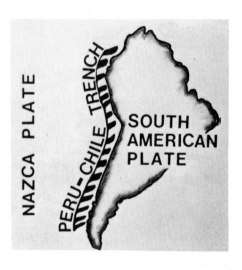

boundary between the plates and within the descending plate. The friction along the crust of the plunging Nazca Plate produces the earthquakes that devastate Chile. The focus for an earthquake can be anywhere along the plunging plate. The focus can be in the trench or under the mountains themselves!

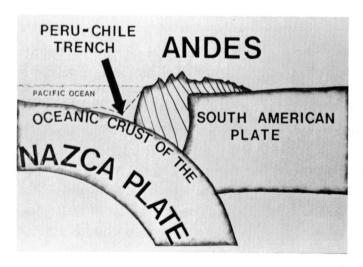

13

HAZARDS IN MOUNTAINS

In the early evening of December 28, 1974, an earthquake shook the mountains in the north of Pakistan. The photo opposite was taken a few days later. This part of Pakistan is a land of deep gorges and high mountain ridges. It is at the western end of the Himalayas. Mountains in this area of Pakistan rise to between 10,000 and 15,000 feet.

Thousands of people were killed as a result of the Pakistan earthquake of 1974. Homes, terraced fields along the sides of mountains, and irrigation systems were shaken apart by the tremors. Great numbers of cattle, buffalo, and goats died. Animals and humans were crushed by rockfalls and buried under landslides.

The Himalayas — the mountains of this region — were formed when the India Plate rammed into Asia. The Indian collision started about thirty-eight million years ago, and we know it is still continuing because the Himalaya system is still rising. Scientists estimate that India is moving northward at a rate of about two inches per year.

When two continents collide, they suture — that is, sew — themselves together to form a larger continent. No one knows where the northern margin of the original Indian

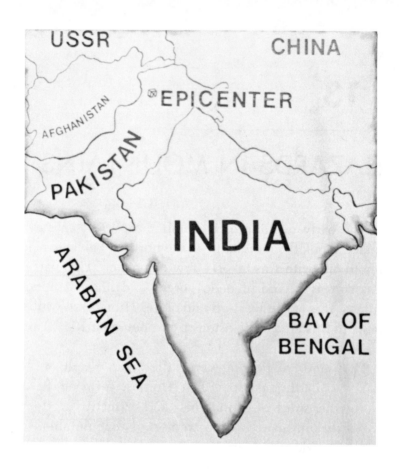

continent lies. That margin has been much deformed in the creation of the Himalayas.

We do know, however, that present-day earthquakes in Pakistan, Tibet, and China are the result of this two-continent collision. The steady northward movement of India is developing a lot of stress and pressure in the region. When the pent-up energy is suddenly released, huge displacements occur. And, as a result, devastating earthquakes are produced.

14

CENTRAL AMERICAN QUAKES.

The majority of earthquakes as well as volcanic eruptions in Central America are caused by the movement of the Cocos Plate. The location of this plate is shown on the map. The Cocos Plate forms a section of the Pacific Ocean's floor.

The Cocos Plate tends to move northeastward, as the arrow indicates. In fact, the Cocos Plate is plunging under the western edge of the Caribbean Plate. A deep oceanic trench, the Middle Americas Trench, marks the border between the Cocos and the Caribbean plates.

The eastern boundary of the Caribbean Plate is at the Puerto Rico Trench. Its northern boundary is also marked by a great canyon in the sea floor, the Cayman Trench. The Cayman Trench extends from between Cuba and Haiti to Guatemala's eastern coast. The northern boundary of the Caribbean Plate continues westward across Central America to meet the Cocos Plate. The landward part of this northern boundary is marked on the map as the Motagua Fault.

In 1773, a severe earthquake demolished Guatemala's then-capital city of Antigua. The region around Antigua

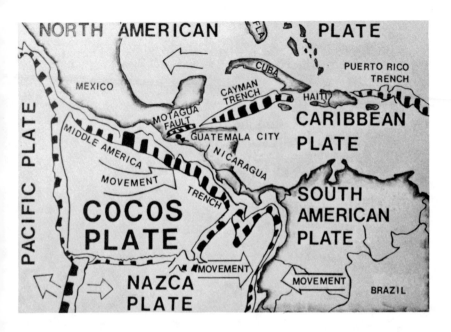

was, obviously, not safe and planners decided to relocate the capital on safer ground. They chose a vast "tranquil" tableland and made it the site of the new capital — Guatemala City. But the safe, tranquil tableland was dealt a major blow by an earthquake in 1917, again in 1942, and most recently on February 4, 1976.

Guatemala City sits atop an insecure footing of thick layers of loosely packed volcanic debris. It is also close to the Montagua Fault. The Guatemala quake of 1976 measured 7.5 on the Richter scale. The death toll caused by the quake was over 25,000.

Three years earlier, on December 23, 1972, movement along the Cocos Plate leveled Managua, the capital of Nicaragua. After the first shock, a cloud of dust rose from Managua to a height of 1,000 feet. There was nothing to see but dust and fires. Earthquakes still rock Nicaragua. One of the latest, in October 1978, registered 5.5 on the Richter scale.

PART
3

Prediction and Problems

An earthquake in a major American city could take thousands of lives. Today, scientists are struggling with three often-asked questions: How can we predict when and where a major earthquake will occur? What will the public response be to such a prediction? What are the best ways to save lives and avoid injuries?

The first earthquake predicted successfully in the United States was a small quake in the Adirondack Mountains of upstate New York. A team of scientists were studying the region. They used data collected by their seismographs to make the prediction. They predicted the event three days before it occurred on Angust 3, 1973.

The Congress of the United States passed an Earthquake Hazards Reduction Act in 1977. About $14 million was designated for prediction studies by this law. Some of the money was spent to develop an expanded earthquake observation network.

Scientists working in this field must begin building long, detailed records. And they must try to identify those events that can be used to predict the time, location, and size of major earthquakes.

15

THE GATHERING EVIDENCE

Until recently, most people believed that earthquakes simply explode from underground without visible warnings. But a serious search for warning signals has been going on for a long time. Russian scientists began their studies in 1949 after an earthquake in Tadzhikistan killed more than 10,000 people.

Russian, Japanese, Chinese, and American scientists have learned a great deal about signals that precede an earthquake. Most of the reported signs are related to the increasing strain within the Earth's crust that leads to a violent break. Some of the signs associated with increasing strain include:

- slight changes in the tilt or elevation of the landscape near the threatened site;
- a change in the velocity of P waves that move through the deep rock in the threatened area;
- a change in the way the crustal rock of the area conducts electricity;
- the appearance of unusually large amounts of a gas, radon, in the water from deep wells in the area;
- changes in the water level or the temperature in deep wells in the area.

16

CHINA: SOME SUCCESS

Scientists in the People's Republic of China have put together a 3,000-year catalog of their earthquakes. The catalog lists 1,000 destructive earthquakes in the last 2,000 years.

Some of the most destructive earthquakes in history have occurred in China. For example, 800,000 people died in a quake near Hsian in Shensi Province on January 23, 1556. The Shensi quake has been estimated at a magnitude of 8. In fact, one out of every sixteen earthquakes in China from 780 through the 1970s has had a magnitude of 8 or greater.

In 1970, an earthquake-prediction network was established in China. The Chinese have had notable success using the network. For example, they were able to predict the Haicheng quake that struck on the evening of February 4, 1975.

The Haicheng quake had a Richter-scale rating of 7.3. More than 90 per cent of the houses in the region collapsed, but very few people or animals were killed. The population of the region—including the animals—was moved outdoors to safe, open areas.

The Haicheng quake of 1975 was predicted principally by changes in well water and in animal behavior.

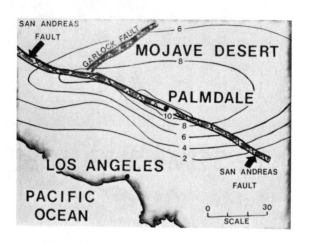

The Chinese report that snakes come out of the ground, rats leave houses and holes, fowl fail to roost at sunset, and dogs bark incessantly before quakes. Some American scientists view such reports of unusual animal behavior with skepticism. Others suggest that some animals may, in fact, be disturbed and alerted by ground vibrations at frequencies higher than we can hear or feel.

Again, in 1976, Chinese scientists announced that an earthquake would occur in T'ang-Shan or possibly in the Peking area. The data, however, were conflicting and confusing. The scientists were unable to make a precise prediction as to place, time, and magnitude. When the earthquake struck T'ang-Shan on July 28, 1976, it caused great havoc and destruction.

The T'ang-Shan quake of 1976 registered 8.2 on the Richter scale. Just before the ground began to shudder and undulate, a brilliant incandescence lit up the dark early-morning sky for hundreds of miles around. As many as 750,000 people lost their lives in the devastation that followed.

17

THE PALMDALE BULGE

Palmdale, California, is located some thirty-five miles north of downtown Los Angeles. The population of Palmdale is about 13,500. It is a small town at the edge of the Mojave Desert. As the map shows, Palmdale sits on the San Andreas Fault.

Studies show that a vast area in the Palmdale region of southern California is being lifted. The area of uplift is known as the *bubble* or *bulge*. It stretches from the Pacific Ocean to the Mojave Desert.

The contour lines drawn on the map show the elevation changes in the past fifteen years. The contour line that encircles Palmdale displays the number 10. This means that the area immediately around Palmdale has been uplifted ten inches in the past fifteen years.

Note the first warning signal listed on page 78. Many studies show that the ground rises noticeably before an earthquake strikes. For example, the ground rose before the 1971 San Fernando, California, quake and the 1964 Japanese quake at Niigata. The Palmdale bulge could be an early warning signal of a major, potentially disastrous earthquake.

18

THE RAMAPO FAULT

A hairline fracture in the ground runs from Peapack, New Jersey, to Stony Point, New York, on the western shore of the Hudson River. This fracture is known as the *Ramapo Fault*. It stretches northeastward from Peapack for a distance of fifty miles.

The Ramapo Fault was very active about 200 million years ago. The fracture is about one billion years old. Compared to the forty-million-year-old San Andreas Fault, the Ramapo is a granddaddy.

Until recently, the Ramapo Fault was thought to be inactive or dormant. But since 1976 at least twelve measurable tremors have been recorded along the fault. Some say the fault is waking up from its long sleep.

Pompton Lakes, New Jersey, is a small community located close to the midpoint of the Ramapo Fault. The town is twenty miles north of Newark, New Jersey. It is about twenty-five miles northwest of the southern tip of Manhattan Island.

On March 11, 1976, an earthquake of magnitude 2.5 on the Richter scale hit Pompton Lakes. The quake's intensity on the Mercalli scale was IV. The shock cracked plaster and some walls in several buildings in Pompton Lakes.

An earthquake rocked the ground for ten miles around Mahwah, New Jersey, on June 30, 1978. Mahwah is located on the New Jersey-New York border. It sits on the fracture at a point about thirteen miles from the fault's eastern end.

The tremors in the New Jersey-New York region run about magnitude 3 and intensity IV. Is there cause for worry? Scientists do not agree on an answer. Some say that the shocks along the Ramapo Fault indicate that a large strain is building up and will relieve itself in a major earthquake. Others believe that the tremors act as safety valves to reduce and dissipate the strains as they occur.

19

SITING NUCLEAR REACTORS

The locations of nuclear power reactors in the United States are shown on the map. The black squares indicate the sites of reactors that are licensed to operate. The black triangles on the map mean that the power plants are in various stages of construction. Nuclear power sites that are in some stage of planning are designated by black circles.

There is a lot of argument and controversy about the threat of earthquakes to nuclear power plants. As you know, ground displacements occur during earthquakes. Obviously, a hazard exists if there is a possibility that a ground displacement may cut through the foundation of a nuclear plant. In addition, there is a difference of opinion as to the maximum shock that may strike in some areas.

During large earthquakes, faulting starts below ground and extends to the surface. At the surface, the shock may abruptly displace the ground by as much as thirty-six feet vertically and twenty-seven feet horizontally. A vertical displacement of thirty-six feet occurred during an Indian earthquake in 1897. A quake in Mongolia in 1957 caused a horizontal displacement of twenty-seven feet.

NUCLEAR POWER REACTORS IN THE UNITED STATES

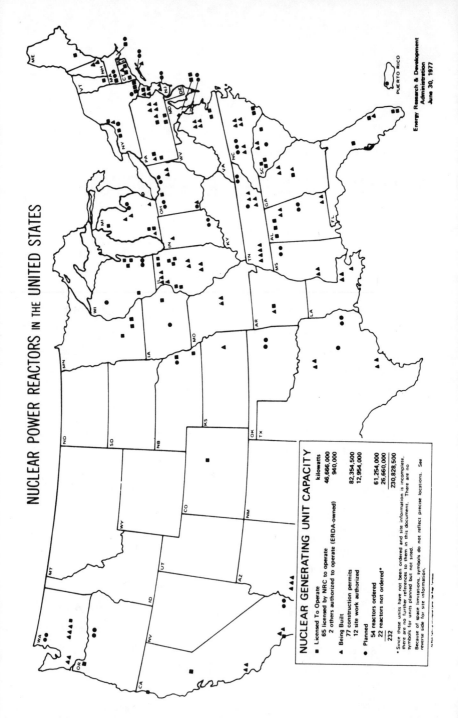

NUCLEAR GENERATING UNIT CAPACITY

	kilowatts
■ Licensed To Operate	46,666,000
65 licensed by NRC to operate	
2 others authorized to operate (ERDA-owned)	940,000
▲ Being Built	82,354,500
77 construction permits	
12 site work authorized	12,954,000
● Planned	
54 reactors ordered	61,254,000
22 reactors not ordered*	26,660,000
232	230,828,500

* Since these units have not been ordered and site information is incomplete, there are no further references to them in this document. There are no symbols for units planned but not sited.

Because of space limitations, symbols do not reflect precise locations. See reverse side for site information.

Energy Research & Development
Administration
June 30, 1977

86

Picking a safe location for a nuclear power plant is an important undertaking. It involves making some difficult decisions. The federal regulations call for public discussion as a site is being considered.

Three nuclear power plants are operating at Indian Point in Buchanan, New York, about thirty miles north of Manhattan. These sites are close to the Ramapo Fault. In fact, on September 22, 1976, a small earthquake occurred under these power plants. Some scientists believe that there is a reason for concern.

No one has knowingly built a nuclear power plant directly over a fault. But, how far away from a fault must a reactor be to be considered safe? Dr. Charles F. Richter, originator of the Richter scale, testified before the Nuclear Regulatory Commission. Dr. Richter said that earthquakes around the Ramapo region are "relatively minor, trivial affairs." Other scientists believe it is possible to have an earthquake disaster at Indian Point!

20

BUILDING FOR SECURITY

The majority of deaths and injuries resulting from an earthquake are caused by the collapse of buildings. Many changes in construction techniques have been proposed to dimish the toll of deaths and serious injuries.

EAM PLANT

In Central and South America, adobe brick made of sun-dried clay and straw is a favorite building material. The bricks are usually held together by a weak mud mortar. Adobe bricks separate easily under the stress of a quake's shock.

Bricks, blocks, and mortar are bad materials to be near in an earthquake. It is very difficult and very costly to build a quake-proof brick house. The building shown in the lower photo, opposite, lost its brick exterior walls during a quake that hit San Fernando City in 1971.

Concrete-block structures can be reinforced by running steel rods down through the block cells and then filling the cells with concrete. This helps to prevent disintegration in a violent shaking. In the lower photo, opposite, the steel rods did prevent the complete col-

lapse of the concrete-block wall during the 1964 Alaskan quake.

It is the strong ground-shaking from earthquakes that destroys buildings. There is no way to completely prevent the damage caused by shaking. The disaster potential in a high-rise building is enormous. Engineers are trying to learn how to minimize the damage.

21

COPING WITH QUAKES

If an earthquake strikes your town, what you do during and immediately after the first tremor may make life-and-death differences for you. These earthquake safety rules may help you to survive.

DURING THE SHAKING:

■ Don't panic. The motion is frightening but, unless it shakes something down on top of you, it is harmless.

■ If it catches you indoors, stay indoors. Take cover under a desk, table, or bench, or in doorways, halls, and against side walls. Stay away from glass.

■ Don't use candles, matches, or other open flames, either during or after the tremor. Douse all fires.

■ If the earthquake catches you outside, move away from buildings and utility wires. Once in the open, stay there until the shaking stops.

■ Don't run through or near buildings. The greatest danger from falling debris is just outside doorways and close to outer walls.

■ If you are in a moving car, stop as quickly as safety permits, but stay in the vehicle. A car is an excellent seismometer, and will jiggle fearsomely on its springs during the earthquake, but it is a good place to stay until the shaking stops.

AFTER THE SHAKING;

- Check your utilities, but do not turn them on. Earth movements may have cracked water, gas, and electrical conduits.

- If you smell gas, open windows and shut off the main valve. Then leave the building and report gas leakage to authorities. Don't re-enter the house until a utility official says it is safe.

- If water mains are damaged, shut off the supply at the main valve.

- If electrical wiring is shorting out, close the switch at the main meter box.

- Turn on your radio or television (if conditions permit) to get the latest emergency bulletins.

- Stay off the telephone except to report an emergency.

- Don't go sight-seeing.

- Stay out of severely damaged buildings; aftershocks can shake them down.

INDEX

JOHN GABRIEL NAVARRA, the author of *Earthquake*, is professor of geoscience and was, for ten years, chairman of the division of science at Jersey City State College. As both a teacher and a writer, Dr. Navarra has an international reputation. He was the teacher of the first televised science course to be offered in the South when he was on the faculty of East Carolina University. He has written a number of trade books for young readers, as well as adult science books, and is the senior author of a complete series of science textbooks, grades kindergarten through nine, that are used by millions of school-children throughout the United States.